The Case

A Three-Act Play

To watch the play, please scan the following QR Code:
The Case

Dr. Sultan bin Muhammad Al-Qasimi

The Case

A Three-Act Play

Al-Qasimi Publications, 2021

The Case - A Three-Act Play
First published in 2000 in Arabic as "Al-Qadiyyah"
by : Al-Qasimi Publications
Author: Dr. Sultan bin Muhammad Al-Qasimi (United Arab Emirates)
Publisher Name: Al-Qasimi Publications
Sharjah, United Arab Emirates
Edition: First
Year of publication: 2021

Translated from the Arabic by: Dr. Ahmed Ali

ISBN: 978-9948-469-57-5
Printing Permission: National Media Council, Abu Dhabi, UAE
No. MC 01-03-7793823, Date: 05-08-2021

Age Classification: E
The age group that matches the content of the books was classified according to the age classification issued by the National Council for Media
----
Al- Qasimi Publications, Al Tarfa, Sheikh Mohammed Bin Zayed Road
PO Box 64009 Sharjah, United Arab Emirates
Tel: 0097165090000, Fax: 0097165520070
Email: info@aqp.ae

CONTENTS

Foreword

Reading the history of the Arab nation, it is obvious that history repeats itself. The similarity between past and current events is stark. In spite of the fact, that play is written from a historical perspective and that the names of the characters, places and events are all real, every aspect of this text is a true reflection of what the Arab nation is going through.

The Author.

Cast of Characters

- History Witness
- Claimant
- Taifa kings
    - King of Banu Sumadih (King of Almeria)
    - King of Ben Ziri, Taifa of Granada
    - King of Banu Amir, Taifa of Valencia
    - King of Banu Jahwar , Taifa of Cordoba
    - King of Banu Abbād, Taifa of Seville
    - King of Banu Muzayn, Taifa of Shilb (Silves)
    - King of Banu Mujāhid, Taifa of Dénia
    - King of Banu Dil-Nūn, Taifa of Toledo
    - King of Banu Hud, Taifa of Zaragoza

  - King of Banu Al-Aftas, Taifa of Badajus
  - King of Banu Hammūd, Taifa of Algeciras (Green Island) and Málaga
  - King of Banu Birzal, Taifa of Carmona
- Voice (1)
- Yūsuf ibn Tashfīn
- Ibn Abbād
- Dignitary (1)
- Dignitary (2)
- King Ferdinand
- Abul-Ghassan
- Sayyid Rami
- Ministers
- Commanders
- Soldiers
- Entourage
- Abul-Qasim ibn Malik
- Ibn Sari
- The Hājib
- The King's Mother
- Abu Abdullah al-Shaghir
- Abul-Qasim al-Malih

- Queen Isabella
- Officials
- Priests
- A Caller
- The Pope
- Aisha, Abu Abdullah's Mother
- Voice (2)
- Caller
- Resistance Men (Ahmad, Muhammad, Abdullah)
- Sayyidat al-Bushrat
- Spaniard Commander
- Spaniard Officer
- Spaniard Soldiers
- Muslims (march group, displaced group, Inquisition group)
- Soldier
- Inquisition Judge
- An old Muslim Man
- Muslims (1-6)

Act One

Scene I

The curtain opens to a wide arena one whose sides are colorful flags for various countries.

A poor-looking man with worn out clothes walks in from one side of the stage. He looks at the flags and the surroundings. In the meantime, an old man with a long beard, holding a cane walks in. He has a large book under his arm. The former man shall be called the 'Claimant' and the latter 'History Witness'.

Claimant: Reverend Sheikh, are you the court judge?

History Witness: Why are you asking?

Claimant: I have a case.

History Witness: My son, I am only a witness.

Claimant: A witness in the court?

History Witness: No, I am a witness to the History.

Claimant: What are holding under your arm?

History Witness: It is History.

Claimant: What use is it?

History Witness: Great use.

Claimant: Could you elaborate? How does one benefit from it?

History Witness: Well, some people did not read it, so, they did not benefit from it. Others read it but did not understand it. These, too, did not get any benefit from it. Still others read it, understood it, but did not act upon the knowledge they gained, and as a result, they reaped no benefit. The only group that benefit from history are those who learn it, understand it and act accordingly. Which group of these are you?

Claimant: I would want to be with the last group as I have an important case here.

History Witness: Well, in this case, let us read the History together.

The History Witness places the book on a table at the side of the stage. At the table there are two chairs. They both sit. The History Witness starts reading from the book.

History Witness: Roman History.

Claimant: No, this does not concern us.

History Witness: Persian History.

Claimant: No, neither does this.

History Witness: History of the Arabs in al-Andalus.

Claimant: Waw! This is great! We will read the songs and the Muwashshahāt.

History Witness *(knocking on the book)*: We will read about the history of a people and their great sufferings.

The Claimant looks around in fear.

History Witness: Do not be scared. This is just history!

Claimant: I know. I understand. Read on.

The History Witness begins to read from the book.

History Witness: In al-Andalus, there was a great Arab state, which was lost because of internal conflicts in the Umayyad family in early 11 century. The State broke into twelve smaller units called Taifas.

Scene II

Three knocks are heard. A voice shouting.

Voice: The Kings of the Taifas.

The kings enter.

1. King of Banu Birzal, Taifa of Carmona
2. King of Banu Muzayn, Taifa of Shilb (Silves)
3. King of Banu Mujāhid, Taifa of Dénia
4. King of Banu Sumadih, Taifa of Almeria
5. King of Banu Jahwar , Taifa of Cordoba
6. King of Banu Dil-Nūn, Taifa of Toledo

7. King of Banu Abbād, Taifa of Seville
8. King of Banu Amir, Taifa of Valencia
9. King of Banu Hud, Taifa of Zaragoza
10. King of Banu Al-Aftas, Taifa of Badajus
11. King of Ben Ziri, Taifa of Granada
12. King of Banu Hammūd, Taifa of Algeciras (Green Island) and Málaga

Shouting exchanges between the Taifas kings. Ibn Sumadih of Almeria advances forward while saying:

Ibn Sumadih: You, Banu Ziri, after you took over the rule of Granada, stsrted your aggression against out lands. You thought your numbers and size of your land would intimidate us. I let you know that we are not scared of you especially that we have the support of those who are willing to help us.

King of Granada: What do you mean you have those who would help you? Are you going to resort to our enemies and the enemies of Islam? By God. We are not afraid of you or your allies.

Another voice shouts:

Voice: And what about us, Banu Amir? King of Banu Jahwar of Cordoba is trying to annex our town, Valencia, to his kingdom. We have been there long before him. He is the intruder.

King of Banu Jahwar walks forward.

King of Banu Jahwar: Valencia is not a state. How are you even qualified to become a King? A King of a town?

Then he turns to the King of Banu Hammūd to say:

King of Banu Jahwar: Listen carefully, Ibn Hammūd, your town is located on the coast and is in control of all our imports and therefore you have subjected our provi-sions to heavy taxes. In Cor-doba, we have no access to the sea. We must have access and to do so, we will take over your land.

The arguing and shouting continue.

An awesome looking man (Yūsuf ibn Tashfīn) walks in holding a sword, which he waves against them. He reproaches them saying:

Yūsuf Ibn Tashfīn: Enough! Enough! You are here fighting with one another while your common enemy is making all the preparations to attack and take you over one after the other?! None of you is able to fight that enemy alone. Your strength is in your unity. It is in your putting your disputes aside. It is in your cooperation in all the aspects that benefit you all. You must know that your enemies will not stop their acts of killing, plundering, and taking over of your lands unless you are united and fight together. You are now divided and fighting among each other while your enemies are waiting for the right moment to seize every piece of land under the control of each one of you. It would be a grave error that we leave or move or be defeated. I have already consulted the scholars and the dignitaries and they are all backing me up to defend al-Andalus, and establish our authority and fight for the sake of its glory, unity and integrity. You also have a great nation that will stand by you, the nation of Islam. All the Muslims will be on our side, supporting us if we are true to ourselves and the cause we are fighting for. They will help us in every possible way when they see in us the spirit of Jihad and the determination to gain victory for the sake our belief. We have to be united; all hand in hand, and prepare everything we can to deter our enemies and the enemies of Allah.

The Kings of the Taifas stand up and offer a seat to Yūsuf ibn Tashfīn. One of them says:

One of the kings: We are all with you.

Ibn Abbād: Brothers, previously I was an ally to Alfonso, the King of Castile, against all my Muslim brothers. I now admit that this was a terrible mistake and I do greatly regret it. Alfonso breached all the agreements we signed together. He also threatened me and all my Muslim brothers. I want to say that from this moment on, I am with you. You are unifying us all and I do not want to be cursed for my alliance with our common enemy. By Allah, I rather be a subject under Sultan Ibn Tashfīn and a shepherd to his camels than be a king subservient to the greedy king of the Christians. I prefer to graze camels to grazing pigs. We are all with you.

Ibn Tashfīn: Now, we can fight our enemies as unified kingdoms. Soldiers, follow me to Zallaqa (Sagrajas) to fight our enemies.

He leaves.

-Blackout-

Scene III

(The Claimant addresses the History Witness).

The Claimant: Who is this?

History Witness: This is Yusūf, the Unifier of the Two Lands.

The Claimant: Yusūf Saladin?

History Witness: No, Yusūf Ibn Tashfīn, the King of the Almoravids. He unified al-Andalus, and then unified it with al-Maghreb. He is the one who defeated the Spaniards in the Battle of Zallaqa.

The Claimant: Then what happened to the Almoravids?

History Witness: Their rule ended at the hands of the Almohads when they rose to power.

The Claimant: The Almohads?

History Witness: Yes, their name was in contradiction with their actions. Most of al-Andalus was lost owing to their actions. Only the Kingdom of Granada and their Kings of Banu Al-Ahmar remained.

The Claimant: They remained to fight the enemies alone?

History Witness: Yes. They did this for a long time until it was time for peace.

The Claimant: Peace?

History Witness: Yes. This is what the history says.

The Claimant: And what happened to Banu al-Ahmar?

History Witness: Let us travel together through time to find out.

-Blackout-

Act Two

Scene I

-Light-

Place: Alhambra Palace, Granada, al-Andalus

Time: Muharram 897 AH (November 1491 CE)

setting Abu Abdullah al-Shaghir's majlis in Alhambra Palace. He walks around with a number of dignitaries, military commanders and Hajibs. They are in groups of two or three; talking and looking very concerned.

One of the dignitaries enters and asks:

Dignitary (1): Where is King Abu Abdullah?

A Dignitary: He is at the Mukhtasar preparing to meet the envoy of the Spaniard enemies, Zafira.

Dignitary (1): All our problems are because of this accursed devil. His treacherous friend, Visir Qumaiha, was a murderer, and he cooperated with his Spaniard masters. Whom is he trying to manipulate now?

Dignitary (2): No one less than the king himself.

Dignitary (1): No power except with God. May He save us!

Abul-Ghassan: I call upon you all to think very carefully before agreeing to anything. I call upon you to stand together in resistance for the sake of our Faith and land. I am prepared to be the first to sacrifice my own life and not surrender. Death in dignity is better than a life of humiliation and cowardice.

Sayyid Rāmi: Abul-Ghassan, my Lord, the King, instructed that a delegation of ours, the dignitaries of Granada, is to go to meet King Ferdinand in order to inform him that we are ready to sign the Peace Agreement.

Abul-Ghassan: That is no Peace Agreement. This is complete surrender! Brothers, I predict that you, Muslims, would be the first to be displaced and driven out your homeland. Do not deceive yourselves into thinking that this agreement is the way out of the problem. This would lead to nothing but the loss of all, including yourselves.

-Blackout and music-

Scene II

(Spotlight on the History Witness and the Claimant)

The Claimant: What happened ...?

History Witness: Well, the Visir and the dignitaries went to negotiate with the Spaniards. They returned with Zafira with documents to sign. They documents had the terms and conditions of the two Catholic monarchs. You will see now how Abu Abdullah reacted when he received the agreement to sign.

-Blackout and music-

Scene III

(Inside Alhambra Palace)

The King appears in the company of Zafira who bows down to the King as he leaves. He faces the king and retreats backward, bowing down a few times, till he is out of the *majlis*.

The ministers and military chiefs surround the king except from the direction of the audience.

The King says:

The King: Do you know what Zafira wanted in this meeting? He presented the Peace Agreement between us and the Spaniards. In fact, I do not agree with this peace proposal. That's why I gathered you today to seek your opinions regarding the Spaniards' proposal.

Abul-Ghassan: Could we see the Agreement?

The King: Yes, the first Article states:

(He starts to read from some documents)

The King of Granada: The King of Granada, military Chiefs, Jurists, *hajibs*, learned men, and religious advisers in the City of Granada and its surrounding areas shall within sixty days from 25 November, 1491, turn over to His Highnesses King Ferdinand and Her Highness Queen Isabella or to their agents the fortress of the Alhambra and the Albaícin with all their towers and gates, and all the other fortress' towers, and gates of the City of Granada.

(Abul-Ghassan, annoyed, objects)

Abul-Ghassan: But, my Lord, this is surrender not peace.

(A dignitary called Abul-Qasim ibn Malik, agitated, responds saying:)

Abul-Qasim: But we are under siege!

Abul-Ghassan: Be it. We can put a very long resistance.

(Another dignitary, Ibn Sari, comes forward)

Ibn Sari: We will starve to death; so will our children.

Abul-Ghassan: Our Suqs are full of food.

Abul-Qasim: Abul-Ghassan, our grain stock has run out. We are seiged. The city has 200,000 inhabitants who are all starving and demanding provisions.

The King: Tell me then what to do!

Abul-Qasim: We, The Granada dignitaries, see no other way out of this but to surrender, Your Highness.

The King: I will not surrender. I will sign a peace agreement.

Abul-Ghassan: My Lord, the King! If you allow me,

I believe it is premature to surrender and sign a peace agreement. Our resources have not run out. There is Egypt, for example. They will provide us with the help we need.

Abul-Qasim: Tell me by God, how is their help going to get to Granada when it is under siege? How could we continue to resist?

Abul-Ghassan: With our arms.

(Another dignitary called Sayyid Rami, interrupts:)

Sayyid Rami: Where do we get the arms from?

Abul-Ghassan: Arms are brought daily to Granada, through the Spaniards themselves.

(At this moment, a Hajib walks in and announces:)

Hajib: Her Highness, the King's Mother

(The King's mother walks in, looking terribly concerned. She looks at her son, the King, and walks round him with a look of despise):

The King's Mother: Surrender? You surrender?

The King: No, mother. I am consulting the Council Chiefs.

The King's Mother: Who are the Council Chiefs? These ones?!

(She points at Ibn Malik while scrutinizing him).

The King's Mother: And who is this? Abul-Qasim ibn Malik?

(Then she points at Ibn Sari):

The King's Mother: And this? Ibn Sari, is it?

(Then she points at Sayyid Rami):

The King's Mother: And who is this? Sayyid Rami?

(She looks at her son and says):

The King's Mother: Where is your uncle who was your supporter? He was murders by such treacherous hands to make way to the signing of this surrender agreement at this lowest of moments … I can see the roads of Alhambra being deserted … with its lights put out. Oh! God!

The pain! The lights of Alhambra are out!

(She repeats this as she walks out and the echo of her words is heard)

The king's mother leaves in anger while the military chiefs stand with their heads down in humiliation and shame. The others who have been accused of treason are fuming.

Abul-Qasim, Ibn Sari and Sayyid Rami advance towards the king, looking extremely annoyed. They keep saying:

Abul-Qasim, Ibn Sari, Sayyid Rami:

Yes, we surrender. We surrender. This is better than losing our wealth.

The king interrupts:

The King: No, we will not surrender. We will have a peace agreement with the Spaniards. Let me read for you the rest of the agreement terms. Where did I leave off?

- After turning over the towers and fortresses, His Highness King Ferdinand and Her Highness

Queen Isabella shall order that no Christian is allowed to climb the wall between Alhambra and Albaícin so that the privacy of the Muslim houses is preserved... Any one who violates this order shall be punished severely.

A Dignitary: By God, these are decent people.

(The King continues to read):

- And to assure secure conditions, one day ahead of surrendering the Alhambra, Abu Abdullah, King of Granada, shall offer as hostages the Hajib Yusuf ibn Coznixa, with five hundred persons, children and siblings of the leading citizens of the city, so that they may remain hostage while the fortresses are surrendered and secured.

- The Muslims party to this agreement shall be treated well, their customs and rites guaranteed. The privileges and liberties to which the Chiefs and Jurists are accustomed under the rule of Abu Abdullah are maintained and it is just that these rights be recognized.

- The Muslims shall be judged under their own laws and courts by the Islamic law they are accustomed to observing, under the authority of their judges.

- If any Muslim has a wife who is a renegade *[a Christian who converted to Islam]*, that person shall not be forced to become Christian against her will.

- It shall not be allowed for any person to mistreat, by deed or by word, any Christian man or woman who, previous to this treaty, has converted to Islam. And if this occurs, the abuser shall be severely punished.

(Abu Abdullah then says):

Abu Abdullah: The terms are too many to read. You can review them when we are ready to sign.

The he calls: Chief, Abul-Qasim al-Malih

(A man walks in holding some papers. The King says to him:)

The King: Come with me.

Both enter the mukhtasar.

One dignitary asks:

Dignitary (1): Abul-Ghassan, what are those other documents?

Dignitary (2): That is another agreement annexed to the first agreement. It is a top secret. It includes all the rights, duties, obligations and privileges extended to Abu Abdullah, King of Granada, his family members and entourage.

Abul-Ghassan: Are we allowed to view it?

Dignitary (1): No, we are not allowed.

Dignitary (3): What do you think it says?

Dignitary (2): Only God knows.

-Blackout-

Scene IV

The lights are on the place where the Agreement will be signed. A table close to the audience with the Agreement document on it. A chair for Abu Abdullah, another for King Ferdinand, and a third for Queen Isabella. To the sides of the stage are chairs for officials from both sides.

The officials enter and take their positions.

A voice calling from outside.

Voice: King Abu Abdullah al-Saghir of Granada

Abu Abdullah enters from the right and stands in the middle of the stage towards the right.

A voice calling from outside.

Voice: King Fredinand of Spain, and Queen Isabella of Sapin

Both enter from the left and stand in the middle of the stage towards the left.

A voice calling from outside.

Voice: The Patron of the peace process, the Pope of Rome

The Pope enters from the back of the stage. He stands between Abu Abdullah and King Ferdinand. They all walk with the Queen towards the table. The pope puts his hands behind the back of both kings as a sign of support.

The Spaniard monarchs and Abu Abdullah sit on the chairs. The Pope starts the signing ceremonies while stretching his arms behind them. The attendees clap.

Inner voice: Sign ..

Do not sign ..
Might overcomes the law.
The agreement phrasing is elegant and the promises are generous ..
Sign ..

It is possible to twist the meaning of the words though ..
Do not sign ..
There are hidden intentions ..
Sign ..
Do not sign ..
Sign ..

(The two parties sign. The exchange copies of the documents. They shakes hands, then retreat; each to his side.)

Ferdinand hands the documents to one of the priests in his entourage, then whispers something to him.

The Priest: So, what are you waiting for, gentlemen? The keys! Hurry up with the keys.

Two key carriers approach holding the keys on pillows. They walk towards Ferdinand who takes the keys.

One Arab dignitary (no. 3) bursts into crying, then quickly leaves while repeating a number of times:

Dignitary (3): *La hawla wa la quwwata illa billah.* There is no power except with Allah.

Ferdinand holds the keys up, waves with them in victory. The rattling of the keys is heard. He kisses the keys, then hands then to Isabella.

The Priest moves (after Ferdinand gives him a subtle look).

The Priest: Come on, gentlemen! What are you waiting for? You need to leave. If you have no keys, you have no place here.

-The lights are dimmed over the characters to a blackout-

Scene V

Light behind the back curtain.

A violent and heated chase is going on. Loud music, shouting, mixed sounds of screams and horses.

-Blackout-

Act Three

Scene I

In Abu Abdullah's bedroom. He is packing. His mother comes in and asks:

The Mother: Where are you going?

Abu Abdullah: Morocco.

The Mother: Morocco? This is how you abandon your kingdom and that of your ancestors'? The legacy of the Arabs and your Muslim forefathers? You surrender in utter defeat!

Abu Abdullah: It cannot be helped! Danger is upon and around us.

The Mother: You should have known all along

that when a merciless enemy is threating a king hiding behind the walls surrounding his fortified palace, the dangers he brings are much more serious than when that king is standing in his military tent in the battlefield. Oh, God! There is no power except with You! Look at me! I and Aisha. A free woman! I am a queen, the wife of a king and the mother of a king. I am a free woman, a noble one among my people who are a glorious nation; the best of all nations among the humankind! Look at me! Can you not see what I have been reduced to? I have become a lost women, destroyed and about to be banished to the unknown!

Abu Abdullah: What is it that I could have done that I didn't?

The Mother: The Arabs are around you. All the Arabs sent you their delegations to help. But you disregarded them all. Instead, so secretly, you met Zafira and dealt with him alone. You agreed with your enemies and went against your loyal allies. You have even surrendered all your arms. What has been left that you have not given up to your enemies? You have acted as if all this means nothing to you. You act at will! Who is going to care for the orphans? What about all the martyrs whose blood had been shed for this land and their faith? This is not about Granada alone. This is a cause for the entire Muslim Ummah! You should have surrounded yourself with men of sincerity and determination. You should have resorted to the strength driven from your Islamic Faith. You should have been in consultation with your Muslim brothers and involved them in this endeavor. When you are then in a situation where you need to sign something, you do it from a position of power where you are able to force your enemy to fulfill their part of the agreement, be it at times of war or peace. You sign when you are certain that your interests are truly protected. Sign when your dignity is preserved. You do not sign until you know that you have free will. If afterwards things go wrong and the agreement is gone with the wind, it would not matter because you would already be in a place of power.

(Abu Abdullah sobs.)

The Mother: You are crying? Calm down! Remember that showing weakness, pain and getting emotional like a helpless mob do not befit Arab and Muslim Kings and Emirs

(Abu Abdullah sobs louder)

The Mother: Well then. Cry like a woman over a kingdom you could not defend like a man.

- Blackout-

Scene II

(After Abdullah left Granada)

Voice: Years pass and Grenada is under extreme forms of hardship.

A group of undercover resistance men waits for the arrival of Sayyidat al-Bushrat (Lady of al-Bushrat). She arrives and looks around checking who is there. She then calls them by name:

Sayyidat al-Bushrat: Ahmad .. Muhammad .. Abdullah. Welcome to the men of the resistance.

(Ahmad, one of the Resistance men removes his face mask) and says:

Ahmad: Sayyidat al-Bushrat! How did you recognize me?

Sayyidat al-Bushrat: You are calling me 'Sayyidat al-Bushrat'! Why that nickname?

Muhammad: for all your efforts in the Battle of al-Bushrat.

Sayyidat al-Bushrat: It is my honour to be called so. Al-Bushrat was one major battle against our enemy where they suffered heavy casualties.

Abdullah: By Allah! In that battle one felt as if he had the strength of an entire army. Your role in this battle was tremendous.

Ahmad: So was the role of that great women-fighters who took part.

Sayyidat al-Bushrat: I almost forgot to give you the arms I have brought with me. There you go, I hid them here.

(Sayyidat al-Bushrat goes to bring the arms which are old-type rifles. She also brings out swords. She hands them the arms and then picks a knife and hides it in her clothes)

Sayyidat al-Bushrat: I am going to keep this knife to use it to defend myself if need be.

Muhammad: Take a rifle or a sword instead.

Sayyidat al-Bushrat: No, the knife should be fine. No one will suspect a knife. They are looking for the resistance men and are using bribery, threats and even torture to get information.

Abdullah: Would your body withstand the torture? Or you would give us up?

Sayyidat al-Bushrat: If I am torn to pieces, I would never say a word about you.

(The voices of soldiers coming are heard)

Sayyidat al-Bushrat: You need to run away before they get here.

A Resistance Man: Sayyidat al-Bushrat, we wish you safety. Good bye.

(Sayyidat al-Bushrat with a sad tone of voice)

Sayyidat al-Bushrat: Good bye, dearest of men! Good bye, purest of men!

(Sayyidat al-Bushrat departs).

- Blackout -

Scene III

- Lights –

(A Spaniard military commander walks onto the stage accompanied by other officers. Soldiers walk about inspecting the place)

(The officer addresses the Commander:)

Officer: Have you not found out the names of those criminals?

Commander: Not yet. However, our intelligence tells us that they are in contact with a woman who knows all about them. If we were to capture her, the resistance will cease.

Officer: So, why do you not arrest her?

Commander: We have just received the information about her and we are now on our way to the town to pick her up.

(A woman's voice screaming at the soldiers is heard when brought to the stage)

Sayyidat al-Bushrat: Let go of me, you criminals! Leave me! Leave me)

Two soldiers drag her; one by hand and the other by hair. She is brought to the stage while shouting:)

Sayyidat al-Bushrat: Let go of me! Let go of me!

A Soldier: Sir, we have found her hiding behind that tree.

Commander: Ah! You must be the woman I am told about. You match the description. Soldiers! Take her away! Torture her till she confesses the places and names of the resistance men.

(The soldiers drag her out).

-Lights are dimmed-

(Sounds of flogging are heard. Sayyidat al-Bushrat screams)

- lights are put up gradually -

(The Commander walks about on the stage)

A Soldier: Sir! She says she would confess.

Commander: Hurry up, bring her in.

(Sayyidat al-Bushrat comes in. Her hands are cuffed and she looks exhausted)

Commander: So, you will confess? If you do, you will not be tortured any more. Go on. Speak.

Sayyidat al-Bushrat: I will. Just tell them to untie my hands, and I will tell you everything.

(A soldier unties her hands.)

Sayyidat al-Bushrat pretends to be adjusting her garment. She gets her knife out, advances towards the audience and cuts off her own tongue, which she then throws away in the face of the Commander.

Her mouth bleeds profusely, and she screams in pain while walking about on the stage like a madman with her mouth open.

The Commander: Keep her away from me.

(A priest enters and he sees Sayyidat al-Bushrat who screams at him, too)

(The Priest addresses the Commander):

Priest: What happened?

Commander: She cut off her own tongue in order that she does not divulge the secrets of the Resistance. I am going to make an example out of Granada for all Muslims to see. I will kill and burn you all. I will not leave a single Muslim alive!

Priest: That would be terrible ... killing without a reason?!

Commander: I have a thousand reasons

Soldiers! Enter Granada and bring me everyone you encounter.

(The soldiers rush out of the stage)

Priest: I am here to hold the Inquisition. I have all the rules that will enable you to punish the Muslims.

Commander: Let us then go to Granada, and start the Inquisition.

-Blackout-

Scene IV

Back curtain lights on revealing a line of Muslims in handcuffs and shackles, driven by Spaniard soldiers.

Spotlight on the Claimant and History Witness.

The Claimant: What is this? Who are those?

History Witness: They are the Muslims of Granada. The Inquisition courts pursued them and ordered thousands of them killed. The surrounding mountains were even called the Red Mountains because of the bloodsheds committed here. The slogan of the Inquisition was "A dead Muslim is better than a living one."

The Claimant: Let time be a witness to this! This is preposterous! History should keep note of this!

History Witness: But this is indeed in the records. *(Pointing to the records of History):* Here. Look.

The Claimant: No, I meant keep record of my case!

History Witness: So, what is your case for me to include in the register?

The Claimant: This is it. This is my case. *(Pointing at the tortured Muslims)* Those are my case.

History Witness: But this is not your case.

The Claimant: It certainly is mine!

-Blackout-

Scene V

Voice *(calling)***:** The courts of Inquisition are held.

The curtains open. A group of Muslim gathering, another group taken to a judge and a priest for trial.

(A soldier brings a Muslim man forward and says:)

Soldier: We heard this man say: "Islam is best and that Jesus is not God, but a Prophet of God."

(The judge deliberates with the Priest. He nods his head approvingly)

Judge: We sentence you to be burnt alive. Take him away.

(The Muslim shouts:)

Muslim: Where are the covenants? Where is the peace agreement?

(He keeps repeating this while being dragged out of the stage till his voice disappears. The judge and priest laugh loudly.)

(The soldier brings another man forward. He says:)

Soldier: We found that this man had his children circumcised and gave them Muslim names.

(The judge deliberates with the Priest, then makes the decision:)

Judge: Death! He is to be executed by inserting heated metal rods through his body.

(The Muslim shouts:)

Muslim: What did I do? Fear God! We have agreements and treaties with you. We have agreements. We have agreements.

(He is dragged out of the stage and his screams vanish gradually. The judge and priest laugh loudly.)

(The soldier brings an old man forward. He says:)

Soldier: We found his man fasting in Ramadan.

(The judge deliberates with the Priest.)

Judge: Death! Death! He is to be executed by crushing his bones. He is to be placed under the thick wooden press whereby his bones are crushed starting from the head all the way down to his toes.

Old Muslim man: You are using these heinous methods to dishonor the Muslims and terminate them. You want the Muslim subjects to live in humiliation and degradation. You want to devoid their homes from any mention of God or Faith; where they cannot raise their voices with the call for the prayer, or even pray or fast or declare their testimony of Faith. You fast as well, don't you? Is fasting a crime for which I deserve to be executed?

Judge: You must leave these lands ..

Old Muslim Man: Let me go. I will leave and will never return.

Judge: No. You are going to be made an example for others. You all will be driven out of here.

Muslim: You will not be able to uproot us from here. Even if you tear us apart, we will grow again, like plants do. We will never leave our home.

(The judge, priest and soldier leave. The gathering remains)

(A man shouts:)

One: They tore the copies of the Qur'an ..

Second: They demolished the mosques

Third: They turned the mosques to Churches.

Fourth: They looted our wealth.

Fifth: They dishonoured us and violated our families.

Sixth: They orphaned our children.

All: Allahu Akbar! Allahu Akbar! Allahu Akbar!

old Muslim man: O, Muslims all over the world. Your Prophet is insulted. Your Qur'an is violated!

Fourth Muslim: O, Followers of Muhammad! We need your help!

Third Muslim: O, Islam! O, Islam! O, Islam!

A group of enemy soldiers enter holding whips. They start flogging the Muslims. But, the Muslims turn round on the stage and return holding a bundle each. The soldiers drive them out while they shout.

Soldiers: Leave this land!

The Muslims turn in a circle on the stage. The soldiers follow them. The Muslims sing:

Muslims: We will return. We will return. We will return. We will definitely return.

- Curtains close -

Scene VI

(The Claimant comes out. He shouts as he goes from the audience hall up to the stage):

Claimant: Wait. Wait. The case. Where is the case?

(He holds the big register)

History Witness: What case?

Claimant: My case!

History Witness: Your case is not here. (pointing at the register).

Claimant: Where is it then?

History Witness: *(Pointing at the Claimant's head)* It is there.

The Claimant *(pensively)***:** Here?!

History Witness: Yes. Tell me, have you read the history?

The Claimant: I did now as I have been seeing it all happen.

History Witness: Did you understand it?

The Claimant: Yes, yes.

History Witness: Then, you need to act accordingly. If you do, you will win your case. Do you understand?

The Claimant: Yes, I do.

History Witness: Then, We will return. We will return.

The Claimant: With the Will of God, We will return.

All sing together: We will return. We will return.

(The actors sing and ask the audience to take part in the singing):

All together: We will return. We will return.

-Curtain close-
-End-

www.ingramcontent.com/pod-product-compliance
Ingram Content Group UK Ltd.
Pitfield, Milton Keynes, MK11 3LW, UK
UKHW021958190726
13853UKWH00004B/1601

9 789948 469575